Saving Tucker

ISBN 979-8-89345-980-7 (paperback)
ISBN 979-8-89345-981-4 (hardcover)
ISBN 979-8-89345-982-1 (digital)

Copyright © 2024 by Kitty Sexton

All rights reserved. No part of this publication may be reproduced, distributed, or transmitted in any form or by any means, including photocopying, recording, or other electronic or mechanical methods without the prior written permission of the publisher. For permission requests, solicit the publisher via the address below.

Christian Faith Publishing
832 Park Avenue
Meadville, PA 16335
www.christianfaithpublishing.com

Printed in the United States of America

Saving Tucker

Kitty Sexton

Once upon a time, there was a little ginger kitten named Tucker. On April 16, 2022, little Tucker had barely opened his eyes and realized he was all alone! Tucker cried and cried for his mother, but she was nowhere to be found. Tucker was very scared as he was trapped in a big excavator!

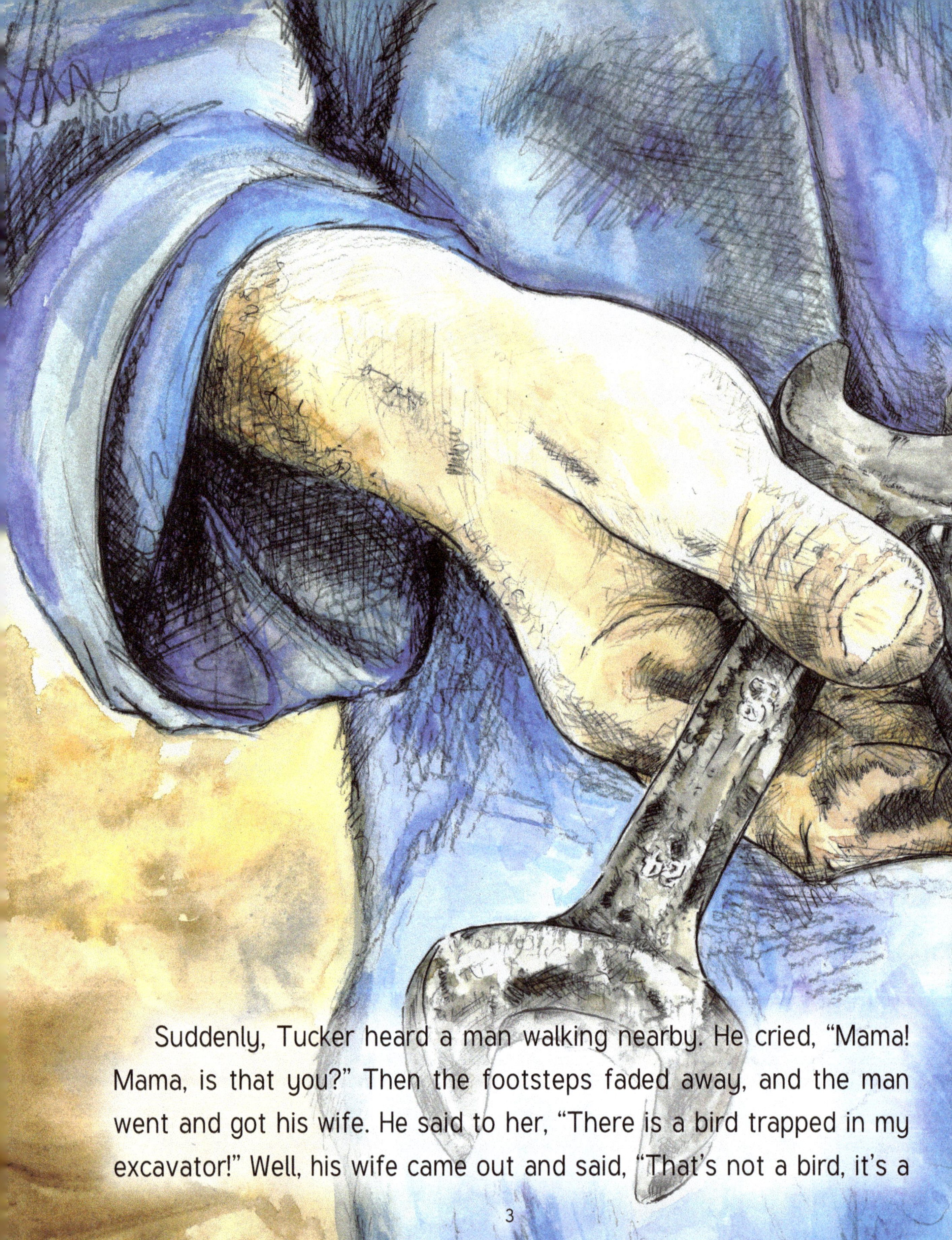

Suddenly, Tucker heard a man walking nearby. He cried, "Mama! Mama, is that you?" Then the footsteps faded away, and the man went and got his wife. He said to her, "There is a bird trapped in my excavator!" Well, his wife came out and said, "That's not a bird, it's a

kitten!" And they started taking the excavator apart to rescue Tucker. The couple searched all over for Tucker's mom, but she was nowhere to be found.

The kind lady took Tucker to the Monroe County Animal Shelter where she knew Tucker could be helped.

It just so happened that volunteer Kit was working at the animal shelter that morning. Kit was busy feeding and watering the cats.

cleaning cages, and playing with and socializing them. "What a blessing," Kit thought, as she did her daily duties. It is a real blessing to be able to take care of the many homeless cats and kittens until they find their "furever" homes.

Kit was still in the cat adoption room when little Tucker was brought in. "Good morning, what have you got there?" Kit asked the kind lady. The kind lady had little Tucker in a small crate and explained how she had found Tucker all alone in their excavator.

"What a cutie!" Kit said.

Kit took one look at little Tucker and said, "This little guy must be about two weeks old as his eyes are just opened. He must have really been scared in that big excavator!"

"Hmm," Kit thought, "a little guy like this requires round-the-clock care with feedings every two hours. I don't have any experience bottle-feeding kittens," but no one else was there to take him so Kit took little Tucker home.

After Kit got Tucker home, she went to the store and got kitten formula and a bottle for him. Kit researched on the internet and found all sorts of help on bottle-feeding kittens and everything Tucker would need. Since Tucker was so tiny, he needed to be fed every two hours! Kit warmed the bottle for the midnight feedings, and little Tucker loved his bottle.

Tucker was so tiny he slept in his crate for several weeks.

Kit brought Tucker in to see the vet soon after she started caring for him to make sure he was healthy and to make sure she was doing everything right. Day in and day out for several weeks, Kit and her husband got up every two hours in the middle of the night to feed him. By May 7, 2022, Tucker no longer needed his bottle, and he was eating canned kitten food.

Tucker loved to eat and play! Tucker ate very well, and he grew and grew! He was also very photogenic! Tucker was so cute he became an internet star!

Meanwhile, Kit continued volunteering at the Monroe County Animal Shelter twice a week, always working with the cats. The shelter is full most of the time, and cats and kittens are always being brought in by animal control or people who find or trap stray cats. On the sixth of May, three little kittens were brought to the shelter without a mama. They were placed with surrogate mom, Phlox, who nursed them for several days. When Kit saw them, she said, "I've been wanting to

bring in more kittens for Tucker. These three are purrfect for Tucker!
They will come in and play with Tucker and become Tucker's siblings."

On May 10, 2022, Kit brought in Shawn, Stevie, and Sammy to foster them and give Tucker someone to play with. Tucker started learning all sorts of important kitten stuff! Tucker, Shawn, Stevie, and Sammy flourished at Kit's house! Tucker was happy to be a big brother now!

Upon their arrival, it was evident that Tucker was very fond of his food. He was so fond of his food he had to be fed separately from Shawn, Stevie, and Sammy; otherwise, he would eat all their food too!

Tucker, Shawn, Stevie, and Sammy loved to play together. They had their own special screened-in "catio," which is like a patio. The weather was "purrfect" at that time of year, and they spent their days out in the fresh air on the screened-in catio. During the night, they were safely tucked into their bedroom inside.

The weeks flew by, and all too quickly, little Tucker, Shawn, Stevie, and Sammy needed to get ready to be adopted. There were vaccinations to get, microchips, and necessary surgeries required before they could be adopted. All four of them headed to the veterinarian for their well-baby checks. They all got a clean bill of health, and then they were all ready to be adopted!

Since Kit had posted pictures of Tucker on Facebook, there was no shortage of applications to adopt him!

EPIC
CAT
LADY

On June 25, Kit's friend was approved for the adoption of Tucker and his new sibling Shawn! Sammy and Stevie also went to loving families!

Tucker and Shawn are living their best lives now and have really grown! They are living happily ever after!

Fostering is so important in providing good homes for abandoned kittens, puppies, cats, and dogs. Working with an animal shelter by volunteering and helping is so important for the success of any animal shelter. It is rewarding and fulfilling work. Kit is still volunteering at the all-new Eastbourne Animal Center, which replaced the Monroe County Animal Shelter. She is still taking in foster cats and kittens!

About the Illustrator

Ed Burley is a lifelong artist on a never-ending quest to create unique and meaningful art. His work spans many mediums, from steampunk sculptures to watercolor paintings and everything in between. This is his first picture book. Ed lives in Tellico Plains, TN, with his wife and their beloved rescue dogs Bean and Britt, two rescue cats and a steady parade of foster cats on their way to forever homes.

About the Author

Kitty Sexton is a retired Air Force veteran Master Sergeant. She is also a glass artist specializing in fused glass. Kit's enduring love for cats, coupled with her fitting name "Kitty," destined her to be an integral part of cat rescue for many years.

Throughout her Air Force career, Kit has been a steadfast supporter of animal shelters across various cities.

Amidst the pandemic, Kit began volunteering at the Monroe County Animal Shelter in Madisonville, Tennessee. As a devoted animal advocate, her passion lies in rescue work. She continues to dedicate two days a week to caring for the cats at the all–new and improved Eastbourne Animal Center.

Kit, originally from Louisiana, is happily married to her husband, Dan, who is also a retired Air Force veteran Master Sergeant. They now call East Tennessee home and are proud parents to their son, Tristan, and daughter, Sarah. Additionally, they have two grandkids, Bryce and Haley. Their household is further enriched by the presence of three beloved rescue cats—Polycarp, Remy, and Sanchez—as well as a rotating cast of foster kitties.

For more information, please go to www.catville.com.

www.ingramcontent.com/pod-product-compliance
Lightning Source LLC
Chambersburg PA
CBHW041822110726
48006CB00019B/2478